Off We Zoom!

by Sarah Snashall
illustrated by Claudia Ranucci

OXFORD
UNIVERSITY PRESS

We load the boxes into the rocket.

We push to go.
We jet off.

We zoom into the air.

Look how high we are now.

We pass the moon.
The rocket zooms on into the dark.

I can see a comet.
Hang on tight!

Now we are too near to the rocks.

Quick!
Keep to the right.

Look!
We are back.
Put the rocket down.

We turn off the rocket.
We go down the ladder.

What is that?

It is Mum and Dad.

Off with the hats.
Off with the boots.

We tuck up in bed.

Encourage students to use the pictures to retell the story.